To Linda

THANK you

Everything, your

friendship and

Support means the

world to me.

Sm So Grateful

to have you

in my life

Andrew. x xx

9 SECRETS TO A MEANINGFUL LIFE

Be the YOU You Were Always Meant to Be

Andrew Dunn

The ideal professional speaker for your next event is Andrew Dunne. Any business organization and corporation that wants to help its employees to become the best version of themselves needs to hire Andrew for keynote speaking and training workshops.

To contact or book Andrew Dunne for speaking engagements and workshops

Email : hairbymane@gmail.com
           dunneandrew@hotmail.com
Website: hairbymane.ie

You can hire Andrew Dunne as a coach and mentor for your team. If you're ready to overcome challenges, create major breakthroughs and happiness in your life, then you will love having Andrew as your coach.

To contact or book Andrew Dunne for speaking engagements and workshops

Email : hairbymane@gmail.com
*   dunneandrew@hotmail.com*
Website: hairbymane.ie

9 Secrets To A Meaningful Life

Be The YOU You Were Always Meant To Be

ANDREW DUNNE

StoryTerrace

DEDICATION

I dedicate this book to my Mom and Dad - my first and most important teachers in my life.

Thank you for giving me this life.

To the most important people in my life, my family. My wife saved my life and my children lit it up more than I ever could have imagined.

Thank you so much, Gib, Erin, Caitlin and Cillian!

Love Dad

CONTENTS

FOREWORD

I first met Andrew in Berlin in 2009, on the night when he was crowned the best colourist in the world at Wella's International TrendVision Award. I remember vividly how I was mesmerised, like most of the audience, by the fantastic look he had crafted on his model that evening. I still recall how deeply I felt that he was someone special as I got the chance to speak to him and congratulate him - an authentic, passionate and generous human being, with a contagious energy, the same energy that we all know so well today. I knew Andrew was someone we needed in the Wella family and that he would be a great global ambassador for Wella in the hairdresser community. Over the years, we have spent quality time together, discussing education and our wonderful industry.

One morning in April 2018, I flew from Geneva to Dublin and met Andrew for breakfast for one of our regular catch-ups. That day, he told me that he had this idea to create an online community that was open to hairstylists from all over the world, where people could learn and grow and become the best versions of themselves. I told him he was on to something meaningful that very few people could authentically champion better than him, and that he had all of the skills he needed to bring this brilliant vision to life. I was committed to helping and supporting him.

Fast forward to today, where the Facebook group 'Wella Professionals global hair community', which Andrew founded and moderates, has over 50,000 members! This amazing community which unites, inspires and educates hairdressers from all over the world, started from one idea and one passionate individual who cultivated it: Andrew. By making his dream come true he has forged invaluable human connections, he has created inspiration and instilled self-belief in so many, ultimately changing lives.

Given Andrew's unique ability to listen and help people from all levels and ages around the world, I was delighted when he told me he was writing this book, and honoured when he asked me to write the foreword.

In this book, there is nothing that Andrew talks about that he has not lived or witnessed himself in his personal journey to fulfilment and success.

My advice:
Read this book!
It can be the lighthouse that helps you every day to stay true and live your most meaningful life.

Sylvie Moreau
Former WELLA Global President

With Sylvie Moreau - one of my most valued mentors!

My salon's first room

Wella community - over 55,000 members in a privately run education and inspiration group. Founded and created by myself.

Wella International TrendVision Award 2009 - First international winner for Ireland!

Wella International TrendVision Award winner 2009. What a moment!

Wella International TrendVision Award 2009. World Color Award Winner!

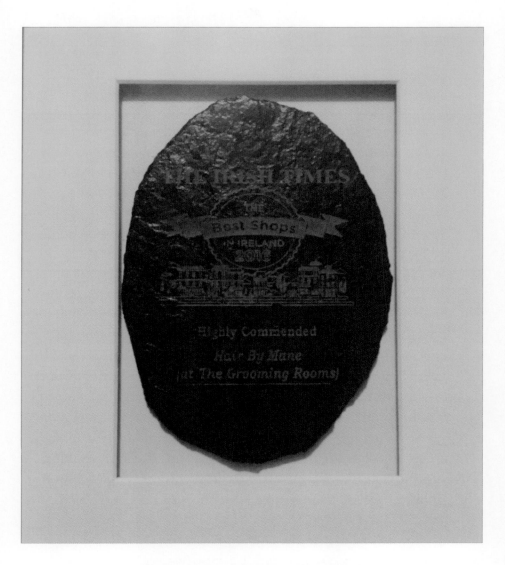

Irish Times Awards - Best Retail Stores in Ireland. It's one of my favourite awards.

My salon has won so many awards over the years. Here are some of them...

The salon being voted 'Best Color Salon'. With my guests of honour, my daughters Caitlin and Erin.

My father Jimmy Dunne - my first mentor

My mum

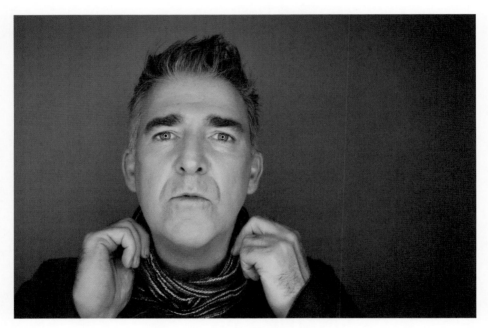

Andrew Dunne

The iconic salon brand: M Mane - Hairbymane

INTRODUCTION

Dear Reader,

Welcome to this book, your book. Within it, are my nine secrets to living your most meaningful life. I would like you to think of this book as a friend you can turn to in times of trouble. It will be there for you when you need it the most, and ultimately I hope to change your life! Read the chapters, do the exercises, laugh, smile and transform.

Please come back to it again and again, whenever you need to. Life is for LIVING and this book, YOUR book, will help you live your best life.

It is hard to pinpoint when I first started to grasp certain concepts and gain understanding in my mind that just resonated with me, and I knew that maybe my mindset was a bit screwed up. I was NOT effective and my mindset was not constructive in driving the processes that I really needed to create things in my life. Not the way it is now, that's for sure. My brain has become a finely tuned machine for creating things, and it is getting better all the time. It just takes time, practice and repetition. It just takes time, practice and repetition. See what I did there?

If you read this book religiously and follow the practical knowledge and wisdom every day, you will realise your own special magic that lies within you. It will grow and grow inside of you. This can, and will, change your life FOREVER. I guarantee it.

Back before my own leap in personal growth and awareness, I became very conscious that I needed to look to the future and create a vision for my life, rather than look back at the memories of the past that plagued me. What I felt specifically on the bridge that day, was the sudden realisation that if I put my focus on the future of what I really want to achieve, and if I worked today to do the things now, that could actually move that future towards me, if I did that every day then it can and must happen in my life. That was a big breakthrough in my mindset for me. My hope is that you will have lots of such 'lightbulb moments' along the way here with me.

I did have a high level of confidence because I had won many international awards for the salon and myself personally as a colourist, I thought I had a pretty good self-image and I was aware that I could be successful in the international arena, but this was a new, DIFFERENT way of thinking. So, I did start to think about the future and what I really wanted, and that did scare me, I won't lie. I realised I was NOT really aware of what my dreams were and of what my real purpose was in life. I just wanted to be happy, but I did not know how to create happiness. I thought happiness was something that just happened for you, outside yourself, that through trying to be a good person happiness would just happen for you. That is just not the case I'm afraid.

Now I was becoming aware that most of the things that were going to happen in my future were rooted in the past, as that was where my focus and mind lived every day, reliving and thinking of my past memories. That was never going to create the future that I wanted! I wanted something MORE. I wanted something bigger. I began to think about what I would really like to happen in the future, what I could do on that day to make it happen; and so change began.

I opened up some major understanding in my mind that day, Unlimited possibilities and potential flowed up from inside me; it was scary yet so exciting. From that day on, things really started to change and grow.

I was also quite successful online, but the community really grew from that mindset of being purely focused on being the best versions of ourselves and creating the future. My social media lives and *Sunday Service* really grew out of that. Being MYSELF really grew from that, and becoming authentic really grew from that. I started to notice that my dreams were no longer like a bird in a cage, just living behind the bars. and that my heart started to burst through to the present. I was a bit afraid at first because my mind was saying, 'Stop, you could fail, is it better not to disturb those dreams?' but my heart was calling me, needing me, wanting me, desiring me to take action, to go for it! The real Andrew was BURSTING through my chest.

That was a massive moment. Literally, I then sort of faced things in the future and was aware of what I could do today that could point the ship (me, my life) in that direction. Then, very slowly, lots of things started to happen. I mean, the best way of describing the inner talk is like this.

Imagine you are sitting in a field and you say to yourself, 'I would love to be able to connect with people around the world. What can I do today to start to make that happen?' Then you plant that idea in a little piece of earth (your mind) and you start to do things to help it grow. The things you do, the actions, are water and sunshine. Trust me, the flower of your true purpose and potential will start growing. This will happen over time because there is a process to life; even if you want to have a baby there are nine months of gestation. If you want to grow a flower, you have to get into the season for the flowers to bloom. It does not happen immediately, but you must keep planting the vision and the ideas. Every day you get a new vision, you get new ideas, you plant them and then every day you walk a little bit more than before and suddenly things begin to happen.

They just happen and will keep happening.

Soon I had a list of things that I had achieved. Some took longer than others, I started to notice that things that were goals and visions before were becoming things that I had now achieved and it felt natural, not even a big deal. It was all just a process, and one I believe we are meant to be doing with our lives. We are meant to be growing and creating, and by following and applying these 9 secrets you will too.

I promise you, just follow this system faithfully and your goals will start to happen for you. You will develop your own system of creation. It happened to me, and if you read this book and follow the secrets I guarantee that it will happen to you.

So, that is a huge part of what this book is about, to move you away from living in and blaming the memories of the past, thinking that the past will create who you are in the future. It does not have to be that way. You can start to look to the future and create a new vision today of what you really, actually want it to be. That alone can change everything.

So in the beginning I really started to look at questions such as, 'Who am I? Who do I like? Who do I look up to? What lights me up?' I was very aware, particularly with a career in hairdressing, that I had a huge need for love and approval, more than say my success and financial gain. Where did this need for love and approval come from? Well, it was something that I had not given myself, therefore I looked for love and approval outside of myself. Because of this I was selling my skills very cheaply. I was selling my visual artistry very cheaply, all because I needed love and approval from complete strangers. That was a massive wake-up call for me, and one that really stung. I became aware of how I sold myself very cheaply just because I wanted people to like me, to approve of me, and I think in hairdressing this is a big problem that we all face at times.

As hairdressers, we are very empathetic people and we want to do the best for our clients. We want them to love their hair, we want them to love us and we want them to love their experience. Because of that, we are afraid to charge our worth. They are the ones going away on holidays and we are the ones exhausted doing 12-hour days, fitting in people who need appointments. So that was another moment when I discovered that the need for love and approval was stronger than the need to actually take care of myself, my wife, my children, my family, my work-life balance and my precious time in this world. Who I was giving my time to? I was giving it away very cheaply. That was a HUGE shift in awarenesses for me, answering 'Who am I?' was massive with my need for love and approval so strong.

We all need to remember that everybody else is taken in this world If we try to be like somebody else on the internet or if we try to win a hair competition by copying somebody else, we will only give a version of somebody else's vision and we will sell ourselves cheaply. We will know it was not our idea, it did not come from us inside. It will not have our magic. Ultimately we won't believe in it and other people will not either. They will know it is not authentically you, or that they have seen this before and you are just doing a version of it. A copy that came from outside of you and not within.

Whenever something comes from you, your authenticity, even when it is being inspired by other people, it will have its own special magic sauce. It will have your energy, your interpretation and your understanding. It is this which makes it so very very valuable. You will become comfortable with yourself. There is only one YOU in the whole world and this book will help you to be and love that person more than anything.

So, I really dug deep into what I loved. What my passions were. What I was skilful at. What I had built up through repetition and intensity in my life to become really good at and what was my value. What would people be willing to pay me for? I found within myself that I was able to help people with their confidence and mindset, and that was very valuable. From finding that out I was able to create from my purpose my *Sunday Service*, my online show for hairdressers around the world. This has just grown and grown. The reason *Sunday Service* really works is it comes from me living my purpose, which is to connect and inspire people around the world, helping them to become the best versions of themselves.

Knowing my actual purpose was massive and another reason why I felt I had to write this book to explain how all the things came together, that you all can start to look to the future rather than the past. When you start looking for and nurturing your dreams instead of hiding from them and being afraid of them, in no time your real self will start to emerge. You can ask yourselves, 'What could I do every day to move toward my dreams?' They can be the smallest things, just little moves, like learning to accept ideas rather than rejecting them, planting and minding ideas and how they come into play, start living your purpose with a focus on who you want to be and what you are meant to do. Is this what I love and where do my skills lie? That's why community is so special and where it all comes from, the beauty, magic and connection of the world, from being online in harmony together.

The thing is, as you start to create little goals for yourself, start with weekly goals, monthly goals, then three-month goals, and yearly goals. But you should always have a lifetime goal, the big dream, the legacy. As you start to make your smaller goals happen you will grow in confidence, and as you grow in confidence your dreams grow with you. So, my dreams now for what I want to do this year are twenty times bigger than they were last year. This year I am talking to you and I am writing a book. If you said that to me last year, that was not even a goal; that was not even on the list.

As you grow in confidence, so will your dreams. A thing to remember, and the thing that I know now that I did not know then, is it is not really about attaining the goal. It is always about the journey, rarely the destination. It is me talking to you now. Please understand, it is the growth that you will experience on the journey towards your goal that makes it, and you, so valuable. It is not really the goal itself. It is the growth towards the goal that makes you who you are. I only really learned that this year because the bigger the goals, the bigger the growth. You know what I mean? So please have huge goals, and huge dreams and that is where you will achieve HUGE growth towards the best version of yourself.

Everything changes when you do achieve a goal. I have achieved a couple in the last few weeks and it just sort of happens, having become so normal to me now. But it is so important to stop, to celebrate that it happened and make something of it, because it brings that positive energy forward, creating proof and momentum. You have achieved your goal because you have pointed the ship (your mind) in that direction and you have worked daily to move towards it. THAT is what this book is all about; having an idea where you are going, pushing yourself in that direction and working diligently every day towards it. Know that even when you reach your goal, which is inevitable, it is the journey towards it that you will look back on and love, that you will remember forever.

Along the way, you will learn so much about yourself, and the difference between real quantifiable fears, and the made-up ones of your mind. The problem is, in the beginning, you don't know the difference but your mind will start to get a little more resilient and get a little bit more accepting that you are always in this flux of change and growth. That there is always a slight level of uncomfortableness in your life. This is good, it means you are growing and that through meditation, living a certain way and doing the right things, it becomes very enjoyable knowing you're always moving towards your goal.

Your mind just wants to protect you. It is afraid that something is going to happen to you. It is an age-old response from an age-old part of your brain. But remember, most of the time when you feel these particular feelings and emotions, it is because you are about to step into your greatness. You are about to step into something that is going to actually change your life in the most beautiful way. The only way your brain knows is to say, 'No, no, no, stay where you are. We are safe here, what could happen? We could fail.' The brain hates the great unknown, but this is just part of the life process and most of the time everything you are looking for is on the other side of taking an action. You need to step into your greatness to create your success. By going through that process you do have to walk on the hot coals of white-knuckle fear at times, but you just have to do it for yourself. Don't worry, you have people in your life like me to say, 'I got you' and we will get through it, together, over to the other side. Have faith in this.

I invite you to hear me in your mind. I want you to feel me in your heart and know that I am with you. We got this! This will all lead you to the life of your dreams. You will learn to do it every single day and it will all happen.

This is my promise to you,
Andrew

Poster for my online show 'Sunday Service' where the idea for my book came from - this wonderful community...

Another one of my famous education days in Manchester.

FEELING
THANKFUL

Hairdressers helping
hairdressers
Wellafamily

*The 1-1 mentorship program that creates a 6-figure-salary's and
7-figure businesses.*

Andrew on the road...

My mum and dad

My mum and dad on their wedding day

My dad, my brothers Gregory and Leslie and myself. Adrian, my younger brother,
was not born yet.

Me as a baby in my mother's arms.

SECRET 1 - THE BRIDGE (AWARENESS)

A day that changed everything ...

One spring day, not that long ago, I was on the bus to work in Dublin as usual. I got off at my usual stop and paused for a moment to sit on a bench just off O'Connell Bridge. It was a beautiful day; the seagulls were soaring above and all around me, the Liffey river was babbling away below, reaching out into the sea, while the bright blue sky was barely dotted with candy-floss clouds. But somehow I couldn't feel it. I felt hollow and disconnected. All around me was life in the fullness of its beauty but I felt empty inside. I was filled with yearning for something or someone I couldn't feel or name.

I have been pretty successful in my career. I'd worked hard for many years, with my head down, focused on the future, rarely taking time to reflect. Whenever difficult feelings came up I drowned them out with anything that worked in the moment and carried on. But that day on the bridge, in all that vastness and beauty, these feelings came flooding in. I just couldn't pretend to be somebody I wasn't any longer.

The truth was my True Self had been calling out to me for years, I hadn't listened and the bottom line was, it scared me. The ten-year-old boy who I'd locked up inside for years was calling to out me. That same evening, when I got home from work, I searched for a photograph of myself as that boy and put him in my wallet; he's lived with me every moment since that day.

No matter what age you are it's never too early or too late to get to know yourself. Remember that kid you were? Well, it's time to get to know that child again. Maybe that child will be a little distant and upset with you because you stopped listening to them and were ashamed of them. Well, don't worry. We will start to heal it all

I only went looking for my real self much later in life. I had built up a level of self-confidence throughout my career, winning many awards for my salon and international awards in my own right as a colourist. I knew my self-image, and I was aware that I could be successful on a global level, but this was a new and different way than I was used to thinking.

So I started to allow myself to look to the future, one I actually really wanted, and that frighted the hell out of me. I had no real awareness of what my dreams were and of what my purpose was. I just wanted to be happy, but I did not know how. I thought happiness was something that just happened to you, outside yourself, when you are trying to be a good person and then that happiness would happen FOR YOU. But I became aware that most of the things that were going to happen were always based on our memories of the past, and what happened yesterday will most likely happen again tomorrow. That was never going to create the future that I wanted. I felt a yearning for something more, something way bigger. Even with the outside success I had achieved, the hollow feeling inside me was always there. I just wasn't fulfilled inside, I know that now.

My emptiness was linked to not living my PURPOSE – then why was I here, why was I on this planet? That yearning that I felt I would try to ignore and cover up with food, alcohol and other diversions. In reality, I needed to look inwards, and connect with who I really was as a person at the deepest level, but I was afraid to do so. I was afraid of the hollowness, that empty feeling that lay there. The sadness and loneliness in my life were actually the lack of connection with the one person who had the power to change it. ME. There was no sense of relationship with myself.

I have since learned you cannot live your best life without having that connection with who you are inside. That's when I discovered the word 'authenticity'. Perhaps it better describes a feeling, that leads you to connect with who you really are deep inside and therefore totally transforms your life.

At the beginning of any change, after the honeymoon period, we do tend to run away from ourselves. We have hidden away for so long, it can take a little while to connect with ourselves truly. The big question to ask ourselves is:

WHY AM I HERE?

On that particular day looking out over the Liffey, I stopped on the bridge and watched over the river towards the ocean. I let the waves of hollowness and yearning hit me. It was so difficult to feel that real emptiness, to feel the overwhelming loneliness and to discover that it was the lack of relationship with myself in the present while I lived in the past causing my pain. As I stood there on that bridge it really hit me. I'd been struggling because I was looking for the answers

OUTSIDE MYSELF.

We all do this and it never works for long as the hollowness always comes back to haunt us. Yet there are permanent solutions if we are committed to embedding them into our lives. By reading this book with me, it will give you the shortcuts and the answers you need, I promise you. From the next day on, after I stood on that bridge, I started to feel myself. I started to feel that little flame which became a burning desire, and through that burning desire came the need for me to teach and express all that I'd learnt. It led me to work online initially and connect to thousands of people there, building one of the world's best hair communities on social media, going live and becoming a lighthouse to so many in lockdown and on onwards. All this has led me to where I am today.

So, today, I would invite you to stop, let that hollowness out, feel that yearning inside you, take a breath and ask yourself:

WHAT'S MY PURPOSE IN THIS LIFE?
WHO I AM SUPPOSED TO BE?

Scary I know but trust me, if you listen and feel for it, you will hear a very quiet voice, a rising emotion inside yourself going 'Yes, I am ... I am here.' Then you'll begin the most important relationship you've had in your life, the relationship with YOURSELF. Your voice and authenticity start and from there on in you'll find you're divinely supported like never before. Why? Because you're in touch with who you were always meant to be since the day you were born onto this planet.

The hard truth is no one else will take this hollowness away from you, no one else will take this yearning away from you, no one is coming to save any of us. We have to come to realise that the answers are inside of us all, waiting to come out. We create everything from within. We can become the creator of our lives. I did, and you can too.

Trust me, please, when I say if you have the courage to ask the right questions it will guarantee you the life you always dreamed of. A deeper purpose will start to grow inside you and all your goals, hopes and dreams in your life will happen. I promise you! Trust me and lets do this together.

All my love,
Andrew

This is the bridge where the book started.

My wonderful wedding day

My wedding day

My wonderful family

Me as a child - a picture I keep in my wallet

Giving one of my famous keynote speeches

It's important to laugh everyday...

SECRET 2 - AUTHENTICITY

Whatever age you are, it's never too early and it's never too late to get to know the real you. Remember the child you once were? Well, it's time to get to know and be one with that child again. Maybe you didn't follow through on the dreams you set for yourself back then. The dreams you had in life and all the things you wanted to achieve. Well NOW is the time to listen and love that child again this will create authenticity and can open up everything for you.

What IS authenticity, really? It is when you are aligned with yourself and what you REALLY need. Remember, everything that you need is already WITHIN you. This we will return to again and again. You don't need to be looking outside yourself, all of the answers are within you.

What IS authenticity? It is being the YOU you were always meant to be. Being the YOU you've always felt you should be. It is about asking yourself the right questions. Who was I meant to be? Who am I? What do I stand for?

Get to know yourself again! You are a really amazing person, unique in every way. The great thing is that, particularly as a hairdresser, when you are aligned with yourself you will attract people who WANT what you have. How AMAZING is that? If you are in touch with yourself and in touch with your magic sauce, you'll attract clients that WANT that magic sauce. That will make you super, SUPER successful. It'll also repel the people who don't want what you have. How about that? A double WIN-WIN! You'll attract people who are in your tribe and repel those that aren't.

How - Good - Is - That!

It's so important to be able to attract the people that you want in your life and repel those that you don't. Authenticity, at its purest, is when you are being the YOU that you were meant to be. To make somebody else's feelings more important than your own is to lose yourself. Lose your sense of self. We all do it, putting other people's feelings, needs, emotions, wants and goals ahead of our own. Over time we can very slowly lose a sense of who we are. We can lose that sense of ourselves. We ALL do it. We can all fall into the trap of believing that other people's opinions are more important than our own. Think about it. Back at school, you had to ask to go to the toilet. How ridiculous is that? Over time we can lose that sense of who we are and what we want and we need to get that back.

What you WANT is important. How you FEEL is important. It is so, so important to get back in touch with this and overcome our need for love and approval. Our need to let others tell us what we want and need in our lives. We must start doing this for ourselves.

To be cool with you - you must get to know yourself. NOTHING else matters. No education, no training, nothing that you buy or save will work for you until you are comfortable with YOU. The inner voice will always be taking over and that's why it is so important to tame it.

What happens if we don't do this if we don't get a sense of ourselves? We'll always look for somebody else's goals and beliefs in life to make us happy and then when we've achieved those things, find they don't make us happy but leave us hollow. Going out and spending your life trying to achieve the perfect weight, the perfect life that isn't YOUR life, but is somebody ELSE's dream, somebody else's goals, won't work. When you get there it won't last. It'll be a fleeting moment in time that won't give you the serenity that you are looking for. You will still be in pain. You will still feel that you are not in touch with yourself. Therefore it is so important, literally life or death, that you get to know yourself. You must know that you are on the road that you are meant to be on and that you know yourself.

Nothing else matters before you are good with YOURSELF.

You must make the commitment to yourself that the sun goes up with you and the sun goes down with you. You must get to know yourself and it is so, so, important that you do. Imagine the pain of, let's say, winning an incredible award or making a huge financial gain and five minutes later you don't feel right because it was never your goal. Never your trophy, never what you really wanted. How sad that would be. Make a commitment TODAY, whether you are five or fifty-five like me, that you are going to get to know yourself, listen to yourself, honour yourself and connect to YOU. Every day try to work on the way to get things started for yourself. How can you become authentic?

What works for me is to do things that make me feel more like me. For me that means study, meditation, music, friendship, exercise, food, and laughter. Find those things that make you feel authentic and trust yourself that this is the foundation, this is where it starts. Nothing can work long-term for you without you having that sense of who you are and that the road you are on is actually YOUR road and not somebody else's.

How do we get started with authenticity? All of the above. Going for a walk in nature helps massively, too. When you start these things, such as meditation, also expect layers of who you are NOT to come up. Your brain will say to you, 'This is who you've been telling me I am for the last thirty years and now you're telling me it's not?' It's going to create a bit of conflict. There are ways you can help yourself through this; I recommend journaling. Your brain is a very elegant piece of work and it will drop questions that you will need to answer. Don't be afraid or run away from this. This is the time to have the COURAGE to stand still and to allow it to hit you. It will not kill you, 'it' is only feelings. You will get through it and come out the other side with a thing that will change your life called GROWTH.

Do all of the above to make you feel more like you. Engage in conversations, too but keep your counsel. This is all about you getting to know yourself. Nobody outside of YOU has the answers that you need. Only the 'you' inside, that little boy or girl, can give you what you need. The answers are right there inside of you. You don't need to go anywhere, you don't need to do anything, you just need to give yourself that little bit of space and have the courage to do this. We can do this TOGETHER.

OK, so how do you KNOW when you've connected with your authenticity, with who you are MEANT to be? That bridge between the hollowness and the yearning will start to connect with the person inside you, the real you. There are some clear indicators.

Number one. You should start to feel a little bit lighter as a person. Think of that age-old saying, 'I just feel a little uplifted today'. That's a sign you've connected, feeling light-hearted. It's a mind and heart connection that means both are in alignment. Your heart is your soul, so you've overcome your logic and reality and you've started to connect with it. That's a really, really good sign.

Number two. You start to feel a little bit more present. You start to look around you and see the trees. You start to see colours and you start to hear those famous sayings people come out with that are highly overused and that nobody understands. You become present. You NEED to be connected to yourself to feel present. You feel that you are 'in the now' a little bit more. You notice dresses, you notice clothes, you notice the blue skies, and you feel that presence.

Number three. You will start to feel the need to serve. This is a very big one for me and the core reason for me writing this book. You start to feel the need to serve, give and express. You start to feel the need to serve other people around you, because you feel that inner gratitude and want to share it so other people can feel a little bit of what you are feeling. You feel the need to express, amplify and grow the vibration of who you are. This is a really good sign that you are starting to lock into yourself and it is an amazing feeling. Don't worry, it comes and goes. You can't expect to feel it all of the time. There are always variations in life, ups and downs, but after a while, you will learn to feel balanced and aligned more than you are not aligned. That's just the way of it.

Number four. You will feel the need to create. You will start to want to do your work and look at it from the inside as well as the outside, saying, 'What if I did it this way?' Rather than copying other people, you will become a creator. A creator when everyone else copies. You'll want to draw from within you, the place where true success lies. Everyone copies, and creators create. It comes from your AUTHENTICITY.

Number five. You will start to feel connections in your world. The right people will start to arrive at the right time. You'll start to be attracted to people who are very much aligned with themselves, people who speak the truth, and you will want to be around them. You'll go looking for those people who will help you get more aligned with yourself. You will be more attracted to your own truth and you'll be more attracted to people who can help you amplify your truth, rather than just giving you the reality of the situation.

Recommendations

Get a journal. You are going to need a journal to use this book. You must be able to brain dump into your journal, remove things from your mind and get them down on paper. Be those thoughts positive or negative, just get them down. Get them down so that you can realign and reimagine. At the very least get a pen and paper. Take a break from logic, take a break from the news, and take a break from other people's opinions about how life and the world are going to work out. Take a break from that kind of reality and test out everything handed with love to you in this chapter. Test it out yourself and find out what works for you. You'll see what works best in your own life.

Get onto it and — this is a big one — never ask the opinion of somebody who isn't living their purpose. Don't seek the opinions of people that live a life that you don't want to live. Seek out the people whose life, energy, clarity and confidence you want for yourself. Seek the opinion of people that you can clearly see living their purpose. It's very IMPORTANT, be very careful who and what you let into your life and unconscious mind.

All my love,
Andrew

SECRET 3 - SELF-IMAGE

In the earlier parts of our lives, we start very early to create an in-authentic image of ourselves. We have to; we want our parents to love us, we want our siblings to love us, we want to do well in school, and we want to survive, so we role-play and see what works.

We do this and we see it helps us fit in and be liked. Say we choose to be a class comedian, because we are funny, or a singer/dancer, whatever works best. All of these different traits are created outside of us as protection against the world we live in. They are very valid and they are much needed. They just become a part of who we are and we actually forget that they are somebody else's view of what we should be. Some of the world's best comedians and entertainers have sadly left the world way too early due to tragic circumstances, mainly because of the level of inauthenticity they needed to survive in their world. It was too far removed from their own reality of who they really were. For most of us, while that gap is never going to end in tragedy, it does limit what we believe and what we really want to do with our lives.

There is the outside image that we portray to the world; our clothes, our weight, our likes, our dislikes, and how we see ourselves, all combine to present an outside image that we have created; an image not unlike a company such as Apple or Nike that creates a brand, an external image that people find attractive and buy into. It is very rare that people have authenticity of their own. It's the place where your happiness and satisfaction will come from. We can never out-earn or never out-perform our self-image. Even if our image from the outside looks incredible; for example, if someone is a bodybuilder, has the most built body and looks incredible. How we FEEL on the inside will determine whether we are happy or not. It will determine what type of relationships we get into, or not. It will determine our whole life. So that understanding is absolutely HUGE.

Strong armour externally is not a guarantee of success. Many people, my past self included, think that if they have the perfect body, they'll be happy; if they get the perfect partner, they won't feel yearning; if they get the perfect job and the perfect title, they'll feel valued and worthy. When these things arrive, based on external armour, none of them matter. You, again, find yourself in that hollow space thinking, 'I thought that if I got this, that or the other than that, this or the other would work.' That's because we are NOT living authenticity with ourselves. It is very important to be aware that your inner image and your inner thoughts are the only things that will really dictate our lives. No matter how much success you see on the outside, you'll see people who win the Lotto and two years later are in trouble, or heavyweight boxers who absolutely conquer the world through discipline and resilience and then, due to a lack of having worked on their own internal self-image, when it's all over have nowhere to go but downhill.

This is a HUGE subject and I'm outlining here the difference between the outside image that we've created to survive and thrive in this world and the inside image, which is the one that we hold of ourselves. If we are truthful, we need to sit down with ourselves and see that it is linked to our confidence. It is linked to everything.

Some of the most insidious things are to do with our self-image. If you see yourself as having been an overweight child, for example, and you've 'been that way all your life', you carry that with you. Then, you lose the weight and keep yourself trim, but on the inside, your image is of somebody who is ten or fifteen pounds heavier. You've gone on that diet, done all the exercise, but if your mind and self-image stays attached to that overweight child, your mind and body will find a way to get those ten or fifteen pounds back. It will fight against you every day of your life.

If you still see yourself as an alcoholic and not as a healed person, your body will find a way to get you to drink again. If you see yourself as not successful and then you find success in your life, your inside self-image will find a way to make sure that you're not successful. It will take it away from you. I spent a long time running from my self-image in my life, thinking that if I ran far enough I could create a new Andrew. Yet no matter how I felt and thought about my new body and new mind, I would revert back to myself, the Andrew I was before, because that is what self-image was. That's what I saw of myself and there was no running from it. There is no running from it, you just have to find a way to change it and alter it. To reframe it and put yourself first.

This is such a difficult one, in the sense that you do feel, 'If I lose the weight, stop drinking, stop smoking', it'll all change on the outside. How you FEEL about yourself on the inside is going to be the determining factor. A lot of the time, when you change how you feel about yourself on the inside it automatically changes on the outside, or there's no reason for it to change because you are quite comfortable in yourself. You'll see that with a lot of people, they are just very comfortable in their own skin. They are not perfect, but they just have a thing about them. They have an energy and a light about them that we are drawn to. This is because they are in touch with their authentic self.

Yes, self-image and authenticity are linked. It is about getting some type of clarity in your life about how you see yourself and being honest about it. For example, running keeps us really busy and it gets us really tired, we keep on running to show we are putting the effort in, but it DOESN'T work! I know, I did it for decades of my life. Trust me here, I'm in my fifties, and I've done more running than most. It just doesn't work. You have to STOP. Have a really good look at yourself and try to put your self-image front and centre. That is what we are going to do in this chapter.

Here's a self-image story for you.

In 2009 I entered the World Vision Colour Awards. At the time, it was the biggest colourist award in the world. You had to win in your home country first, then you went on to represent your country against other countries from around the world. It was a HUGE contest and there were massive competition budgets for these kinds of shows. I entered and I was expected to win the Irish one because I was already a hugely experienced colourist, I was probably the best, if not THE best in my particular area of Ireland. To a certain extent, it was already a risk for me to enter because I had built up a profile, but I felt it'd give me an opportunity to get to the Worlds and I already had a BRILLIANT idea that I thought could really do well.

There's no point in entering these things unless you have some type of INSPIRATION and an IDEA of what you want it to look like, what you want your vision to be. It goes back to goals and you need to have that. I had that. I had a very specific idea and the right girl turned up.

It's a really long, long competition. You enter for Ireland and get ready for Ireland which takes a whole six months. Then it's another three months to prepare yourself to represent Ireland at the Worlds. For me, it was always about the Worlds. Even though everyone thought I was mad, I knew I had a good chance that if I got to the world with the right model, I had a really good chance of winning. All good on the self-image front. But, as you know from what you've heard already, you can't outrun your self-image, you can't out-earn your self-image and you can't out-live your self-image. If you feel that you are a fifty thousand-a-year person, then that's what you will be. Regardless of the fact that when someone gives you a job where you are on five million a year, you will find a way to sabotage it because you will always work to the limitations of your belief systems within your brain. ALWAYS.

You can't outrun a bad self-image. It doesn't necessarily have to be about body image. It's about your self-image.

For me, the competition was about a self-image upgrade. There were challenges all along the way. Challenges with clothes, challenges with make-up, just so many challenges along the way that meant I had to come UP and really believe in my self-image all the way.

I won the Irish competition.

On the day of the 2009 International final in Berlin, I knew that I was in with an opportunity to win this. Yet my unconscious mind, my self-critical voice was so strong that particular afternoon. Even though it was judged and I knew by that time we were one of the favourites to win that night, the voice in my head, the voice of my self-image was saying to me, 'Who do YOU think you are to THINK that you have the right to win this competition?'

I was curled up in a ball of anxiety in my hotel room, hounded by this voice in my head. I was so CLOSE to an upgrade, so CLOSE to a change. That voice was so real to me, I just didn't think I could overcome it. It was a GIGANTIC voice. That day, I just prayed to my dad, who'd passed away, saying, 'Dad, I don't wanna come second or third, I wanna win this. I want to come FIRST!'

That declaration to my dad got me through. That evening I went on to win the International Global Colour Award, the first Irish person to ever do so. I woke up the next day and was thinking about these huge, colourful scarves that the best hairdressers wear. I say wear; drape themselves in would be more like it. My self-image told me I wasn't that type of person. I didn't feel worthy enough. Up to that point.

The next morning at the hotel after my win, I went out and bought myself a HUGE scarf. I looked at myself in the mirror draped in this thing and I knew, I knew at that moment, that my self-image had changed. That voice was turned down a couple of decibels, drowned out perhaps by the loud scarf. That was when I knew that the voice in my head was not actually me It was just an accumulation of different people throughout my life that had created my belief system. But there was actually somebody behind that voice. That somebody was the REAL person, the real me. It was one of my first self-image upgrades.

What is YOUR self-image going to be? What is your competition and what is your scarf?

Let's have some questions about YOUR self-image. How you see yourself, not how others see you. How you speak to yourself and the limitations we all live under. Until we don't. They are so ingrained in us from such a young age that they are difficult to spot.

Question One: What do you think about YOU?

What do you think about yourself? Sit down with a piece of paper and answer this REALLY carefully.

Question Two: What are you LOOKING for?

You need to be very clear and concise about what you are looking for because it is most likely that the thing you are looking for is yourself. YOU. We attract what we are looking for, deep down, but we cannot find it because our limitations are blocking us. Our belief systems say, 'Oh well, that wouldn't be for me. I wouldn't be the type of person that would drive that type of car.' We block it, but it's not true. You are that type of person. That type of person that does deserve that type of car, that type of house.

Ask yourself what you are looking for, because what you are looking for is most likely looking for you, too. The only thing stopping you from getting it is YOU.

Question Three: How can you see yourself as you want to BE?

Healthy, happy, wealthy. How can you see yourself as that person NOW? By seeing yourself as that person now, you, in time, will become that person. You'll attract it towards you. You have to be prepared to sit down with yourself and say that you are willing to let go of the old you. Are you willing to take the lead role in the movie of your life and not just be a bit player? Are you willing to have the adventure of YOUR life? Not somebody else's life, yours.

What do you need to let go of in life to do this? There are so many things we have to reframe in our minds that we use to block ourselves. Terrible traumatic experiences we've been through and we have to find the good in them, put them to sleep, and get comfortable with them. We HAVE to for ourselves so that when we look back we don't see the drama, don't feel the emotion. It is LONG gone. When the cells in your body die and regrow every seven to ten days, such experiences are long gone on a cellular level. It is only the memories that we keep rehashing. We must make peace and find the good.

If you can reframe the memory, you can reframe your life. You have to be willing to reframe that inner spiel you have in your head. An actor, taking on a role, has to BECOME that person. In a sense, you have to become the person that you were meant to be, NOT the limiting role you have that was created through awful experiences, none of which were your own fault. It's just the stuff of life, stop blaming yourself. Now is the time to TAKE control, to create the self-image that is deep inside you that is absolute perfection, to reach out to what you want to achieve and to start working towards it.

Exercise

Write out a self-image statement of who you are from the most positive place you can. Start it with I AM and off you go. Remember, writing it brings your focus understanding and imagination into the present moment, It impresses your beliefs onto your subconscious which is where your self-image resides. The more difficult this is, the more aware you are of how far you are from the image of who you are meant to be. Then you can start to become the person you were always meant to be. Write this script daily for one month in the beginning. It is time to become the self you were always meant to be.

With love,
Andrew

SECRET 4 - UNDERLYING BELIEF SYSTEMS

We ALL have them. Every single one of us and We are going to work on them together ok. Belief systems are very sneaky because we don't believe that we have them, half the time. Let's take our time with this one and write down some limiting beliefs that you have about yourself. I can start us off. No problem on that one! I thought that I was not good enough, not smart enough, not worthy – certainly not worthy! – unable, for example, to write a book, like I'm doing now. These were all limiting beliefs that I was living with.

Do take your time and write down your own.

The thing to remember here is that, regardless of what is going on in the outside world, whatever our limited beliefs are telling us, our mind goes searching for evidence of it. So while on the outside I might say, 'I'm going to write a really brilliant book. It's going to be amazing and millions of people are going to buy it', if inside I'm saying to myself, 'nobody is going to buy my book, it won't be good enough' my mind is going to go looking for the evidence that nobody will buy it and it's not good enough. In fact, as I'm saying it, my mind has probably found the evidence for this already. Isn't that just life-changing? Isn't that just life-thwarting?

Whatever you say externally, it makes absolutely no difference unless it has changed inside of you. Whatever you believe, your mind will find evidence for. That's its job. If you believe that you aren't good enough, your mind will go searching for evidence to prove that you aren't good enough. That is your mind's job. That is what your mind MUST do.

You can say on the outside, 'I am worthy', but if you don't believe this inside, your mind will look for evidence of it. This radical new way of thinking will change your whole life. Literally. You can't change ANY of your life without it.

The number one thing about limiting beliefs is that you must recognise them. See them when they're happening. 'Oh, no, I'm not good enough.' That's a limiting belief. Spot it immediately. Call it out. Tell yourself that it isn't true. I am MORE than good enough. I'd advise getting a piece of paper; you'll have limiting beliefs all the time. Be aware of them and recognise them. Say no to them, call them out and kill them. Cancel them. Have no time for them. Then reframe them. To show the best way to do this, let's use me as an example again: 'Nobody wants to read what I have to say and nobody will want to buy it'…

Let's call that out RIGHT now. That's not true! There are over fifty thousand people in the Wella Hair Community, people watch my live 'Sunday Service' in their thousands, I've helped many people who have contacted me to tell me so. Many, many of them. I have a level of wisdom, I'm in my fifties. I have an authenticity that chimes with people and I feel I can have so much more to give to them.

That's me reframing that I'm not good enough. By doing that, I am creating the duality and bringing it around. What you need to do with these underlying beliefs is change them. Write down what is ACTUALLY true and your mind will then go and look for evidence to support it. Go and look for evidence that you have a LOT to say, look for evidence that you are wise, and look for evidence that you are smart. Your mind will go off and find evidence for your SUCCESS instead of evidence for your FAILURE. It ALL comes down to your self-talk. You must recognise when you are taking yourself down, recognise it, kill it, call it out and STOP it IMMEDIATELY! Then you must REFRAME it.

Another good example for me could be if I wrote down that I wasn't good enough to write a book. I'm dyslexic, for a start, so I'd already be finding evidence that I couldn't write a book. Straight after that, I'd write in BIG letters:

BULLSHIT

You see, even though I've misspelt it, I know that I'm more than capable of writing a book; that's what copy editors are for.

BULLSHIT

See!

I got people to help me, I learned, I grew, I expressed, I have a voice, I'm authentic, I have a lot to say, I can help people and I already do help people around the world already, it's evidenced that I've helped thousands of them, so THAT is the truth. I've reframed it. So you see that the idea is the brain will always look for evidence of the statements that you give it. If you have underlying 'I can't do this, that and the other', your brain will go looking for evidence of it. You must recognise it and cancel it.

Then, what I like to do is the bullshit test. Put your underlying beliefs down on paper. 'I'm not good enough because...' etc., get it all down. Then write BULLSHIT followed by the opposite of all of these negative underlying beliefs and your brain will go looking for evidence of that success. Do that and you can change your whole life. There will then be very few things that you won't be able to do, because rewriting your underlying belief systems is rewriting your life. Reframe your thoughts and change your whole life.

For goal setting to work, there are a lot of moving parts that you need to put together. They will give you the momentum to get your mindset going, and get your brain moving in the direction that makes you an everyday unstoppable force towards what you want to achieve and how you want to achieve it.

The next moving part is strategies. You need to look at strategies that will get you there. Nobody knows your strategies better than you do, nobody knows your goal better than you do. Usually one looks to have five or so strategies and employ the S-M-A-R-T system. The letters in the system stand for particular words. 'S' means is it Specific, in other words, are you very specific about how you're going to get there? 'M', is it Measurable? Can you measure your progress daily? Is it something that you can do daily that moves you towards your progress? 'A', is it 'Attainable'? Is what you are trying to do a good progressive step, or is it a quantum leap? Whichever direction you are going in, is it attainable? Each one of your steps needs to be small enough that you can reach it so that you can keep moving forwards. 'R', is it 'Realistic'? Realistic so that you can build upon what you have already done and create something achievable for your next step. Finally, 'T', is it 'Timely'? In other words, put a date down on it and stick to it.

Success leaves clues and these are the clues for success right here; strategies like a shift in mindset, and being able to change your underlying beliefs. These are all the clues that you need for success. Follow the clues and we, together, will be successful. Successful people, when they are developing specific measurable, attainable, realistic, timely wins, tend to become even more successful. People whose ways of working are not realistic, not attainable, and not timely, have a tendency to fail. They fail more regularly because everything starts with your beliefs and your mindset. It all starts with the way you've set yourself up.

This is **REALLY** important, the meat and potatoes of getting things done. This book is a book on inspiration and aspiration, but it's also a book of how-to, a book of action. Please carry these actions out. Is it specific, is it measurable, is it attainable, is it realistic, is it timely? These are the strategies that will re-engineer you to the work which needs to be done, and help you with the LARGEST of large moves, making them ATTAINABLE. You'll just find yourself ticking boxes off.

Another great thing to do is to write yourself a LETTER. Write a letter to your future self, a year from now, after you have achieved your goal. How will you feel, knowing that you've achieved it? How is your life now? How different is your schedule? Are you living in the same house? Are you driving the same car? Are you in the same job? Consider all of the aspects of your future goal. Imagine yourself AFTER achieving your goal. It's a great way to do it. You can write yourself a future letter. For example:

Dear Andrew,
I'm reading this here today and I can't believe that I'm standing on a stage in front of thousands of people…
Love Andrew

Think about what your goals are and be specific. It's a good thing to write this letter to your future self, keep it in your wallet or handbag and read it to yourself once or twice a week. It's a little declaration to yourself. It will keep your mind constantly focused on what you want to achieve. Your brain will be looking for evidence to prove yourself right. Your brain, mind and spirit will rise to the idea and set about ways to achieve it.

All very workable strategies. Very workable by YOU.

With best wishes,
Andrew

SECRET 5 - GOAL SETTING

A great analogy to think about when beginning to look at goal setting is the idea that you would never really leave your home, get into your car and just drive aimlessly. You wouldn't do this without knowing that you had a destination in mind. The better the destination you have chosen and how it makes you feel thinking about getting there, the better the drive is going to be.

Our lives need to be approached in the same way as that drive. If you wake up every day and you are not working towards a goal or a couple of goals, you won't get very far, I would recommend that you have a couple of goals, otherwise it is really hard to know if you are making progress. You need to know that you are getting somewhere. The idea of having a goal is always the GROWTH that you gain on the way to the goal. The journey is as important as the destination. The journey to the destination can make you enjoy the destination even more. For example, the road to fame is more fun than fame itself. Being on the road, building yourself up, having that target and waking up every day with that desire to be successful, to be the best in the world at what you do. Your DESIRE gives you the fuel. Without your goal, you don't have the desire and without a proper goal, a REAL goal, a goal that scares you a little bit, one that you aren't totally sure how you're going to achieve it, you are missing the sauce that makes life so magical. Life can be tough. You will face resistance. It can and will knock you down. Your goals, your dreams and your desires will pick you up and teach you to fly!

Stuff just happens in life, as reliable as the weather, so having a goal will set your natural GPS, which is your mind. Your desire will always be fuelled by your daily practices; they will move you towards your destination every moment of every day. Along the way you could make a couple of stops, you could get lost, and the journey could be filled with some difficult roads, snow and ice. But on each part of that journey, you'll know, every morning, where you are going and how you are going to get there. This is why goals are so, so important.

I like to have weekly goals, three-month goals and yearly goals. I like to have really big goals. This is what we are going to be looking at in this chapter. You have to be able to sit with yourself and allow yourself to daydream a little bit. Get back to that time, before you went to school and you were then forced to stop daydreaming. Stop looking out of the window and get back to your schoolwork! How wrong they were. We have to allow ourselves access to our imaginations and to daydream. I give you permission to ask yourself today the most beautiful question:

WHAT DO I REALLY WANT?

Sit back now and allow yourself to think about it. Let yourself dream, create and feel. Let go of the part of your brain that says, 'I don't think I can do that', or, 'I'm too old'.

Just let go of all that and simply ask yourself, am I able to do it?

Of course, you are! You are able to do it, you just don't know how, that's all. They are not the same thing. If you are able to do it, then get on the road towards it and the road will show you how. Don't worry about the how, worry about the why and think about the desire. Imagine how it's going to feel when you get there. Be sure that you are willing to pay the price. Every journey is heading towards a destination. Are you willing to see it through?

Failing isn't failing, failing is just feedback. The only failure in life is quitting. The only failure is giving up. All you need to know is that you are working towards your goal day by day, week by week. This comes from inside of you. You are working towards your goal from inside yourself. Every single day. But, if you don't know where you are going, imagine trying to drive without a destination. You move TOWARDS the place you want to be, you take the required actions. You know that your thoughts are things, your thoughts are energy. So, every day, you focus on your goal. Every day you think about your goal. Every day you obsess about your goal. Every day you aim towards it. It's not that you want to rush the process, there's no need to speed it up. Touch it, feel it, smell it. Imagine yourself as a part of it.

Know that the journey towards your goal is going to make you the person you need to be, one that is able to attain that goal. It is the JOURNEY that you will never forget. The journey will see you encounter and overcome resistance. There will be good times, tough times, battles and wins along the way. You'll be able to look back and love it all! Such is the way to live. This way, magic happens all the time!

Just a couple of weeks ago I had two HUGE goals that I'd ticked off in the space of a few days. Firstly, I was on stage and I saw my picture and the word 'global' in the title on huge screens both behind me and in front of me. Wow! This was part of a goal that I'd been working toward for well over a year, and here it was happening to me! I now have completely different goals; I had already moved and grown as a person to become what I wanted before it happened. I was that person, and seeing the title just let me know the change had already happened, slowly and perfectly over time. See? Once you've finished a goal, you will have a new one. It's a never-ending process. It's what keeps your heart alive and your body active. Always having goals means you will always be growing as a person, inside and out.

If your heart and mind are aligned with your goal, it doesn't matter if you are eight, thirty-eight or eighty, they will keep you going towards that goal. That will keep you healthy, keep you well, keep you eating the right foods and doing the right things. You will be taking care of yourself because you want to achieve things in your life. Your goals are SO important. I cannot emphasise this enough. If you don't have a goal, you don't have a desire and you don't have a map or a journey. Whether your goals are monthly, annual or HUGE, you need to have ones in place that light your fire and get you out of bed in the morning.

Goals are the reason that you are here. You have to set yourself up for success in your mind, to be able to get to where you want to be. So, once you've allowed yourself to dream the things that you'd like to achieve in your life, you now need to start to work in the NOW. Work in the present. It is in the present moment, the now, that the future is created. Daydream always (as your achievements all start there in your mind, your imagination always) then come back to the present moment and work from there. We must always have our dreams in our hearts and minds, and from there, we need to say to ourselves, 'Who do I need to BE in order for me to make this goal and success HAPPEN? Who do I need to be to create this?' Then watch how you grow as a person to match your dreams. I promise you will.

For me, Andrew, I'm a mentor and a coach. I'm someone who hopefully inspires and lights up as many people as possible every single day. I'm also a fantastic colourist. So, who do I NEED to be to create this reality? I need to be confident, I need to be wise, I need to be able to grow as a person every day, I need to be special, I need to be a leader and I need to be charismatic. I need to be and have ALL those things.

Most people think that they have to go out and get all of those things before they can achieve their goal. But that is the wrong way around. You need to say to yourself, who do I need to BE, and then you just need to STATE it and BECOME it. It's an awful lot easier than people make it out to be. You just ask yourself what and who you need to be every day.

What I do is say to myself that I need to be confident, wise, a leader and charismatic. Then I switch the word BE with the words I AM.

I AM are two small but huge words that have been used throughout time which bring you back to YOU, to the real power in life. The REAL power which starts with YOU, starts inside you. All energy changes when you change. All of your life changes when you change. Everything comes back to a focus on I AM.

I could say, 'I am confident' (which I am), 'I am wise' (which I am), 'I am growing every day', 'I am charismatic', 'I am a leader' (all of which I am). In doing so I go from who I need to be to who I am. You will do that too.

These are the first two elements of your goal creation that you need to be able to work with. After you've worked on creating your goal, you work on who you need to be to create this goal. Who do I need to be, what do I need to do? Then say, I am.

Say them, feel them, mean them and you will BECOME them.

Once again. Say them, feel them, mean them and you will BECOME them.

It is SO important that you get your inner dialogue with yourself RIGHT.

The way we mostly talk to ourselves is awful. We wouldn't talk to a DOG the way that we often talk to ourselves. We can be our worst critic, our worst enemy. We need to take that voice on before we take on anyone else's voice. NO voice outside your head is as critical as the one inside your head. NO voice outside your head is going to tell you that you can't do it as much as the voice inside your head. The only real battle you will fight is with the wrong and terrible judgements we make in our own minds

We must start there and know that voice is an accumulation of all the negative external opinions and judgements over the years. It most definitely ISN'T you. I will say that again; it is not you. It's stuff you've been accumulating from the age of two, from your ancestors, but please remember from now onwards it isn't you.

So, we start by asking, 'Who do I need to be in order to achieve this goal?' Who do I need to be to create this success? Who do I need to be to get to that goal? I need to be confident, charismatic, wise and a leader. Ok. I am, I am Andrew. I AM. Say all those wonderful things to yourself every day. I AM. It's such a strong phrase. It broke and rebuilt me, and it will do the same for you. So say out loud, I am confident, I am wise, I am growing every day, I am special, I am a leader. I AM.

Everything starts with who you need to be,
and then you move into 'I am'.
Who do you need to be?
What 'I am' will you become?
It is time.

Go for it.
Your new YOU awaits you,
I will see you there,
Andrew

SECRET 6 - DAILY PRACTICES

In this chapter, we will look at the things that we can do every day to help our mindset and keep us positive. The key to changing core belief systems is repetition. I'll repeat this; the key to changing core belief systems is constant REPETITION.

Whatever you do, if you start something new it will take time and practice to overcome the old ways. It's like learning to drive. If you keep having to learn new ways of driving, it will take a while for them to become habitual, to become unconscious. You can change bad driving habits by consciously changing them, then repeating them until they become unconscious behaviour and just natural movements.

It will take lots of REPETITION and good focus matched with INTENSITY to create change. So daily practices are hugely important. You cannot and will not be able to change your mindset unless you approach things from an everyday, daily practice perspective. You spend your whole life creating a bad belief system that does not serve you. It does not help you to get to where you want to go in life. You can, however, replace this mindset.

It has been discovered that when you were pre-school age, belief systems were implanted by your parents or the schoolyard. They are not your core beliefs at all but were imposed on us by the judgement and opinions of others, I'm afraid, and once we aligned to them emotionally they became a part of us. None of this was done on purpose at all, the same had just happened to the responsible adults in our lives; they believed their core values to be true and so they passed them on. We do it ourselves too, sadly. But now as self-aware adults, you must take responsibility for your own beliefs, if you want to be successful. You must change the mindset and beliefs that block you. They cannot be changed just once, they cannot be changed just twice. The techniques to change need to be practised thousands and thousands of times.

Why is change a daily practice? We have spent most of our lives telling ourselves that we are just this way because of XYZ, such as, 'I'm just slow', 'I'm from a family that naturally puts on weight', 'We're all dyslexic', 'We all have drink problems', or 'We all eat too much'. These are all just belief systems, none of them are actually real, and with the knowledge and awareness of this you have to ask yourself, 'IS it true?' But then, what is true really?

Yes, what is really true in life? It is only what is of value to you and your life. The hard truth is. that if your mindset and belief systems are of no value to you and if they aren't helping you go where you need to go, then you need to replace them with a new mindset. That will take time, focus repetition and desire. Remember, nothing in life wants to die, including your old belief systems! You've spent a lifetime creating these brain patterns after all. But we need to STOP looking for answers and stories from the past.

We need to just put them down. I know how. difficult that sounds but it isn't, it just takes time practice and constant repetition.

It is time to create NEW beliefs and fully focus on our future. It is time to start to create it now, little by little. You can start to become a future-forward person, who through the beliefs that you create today, can go on and make new beliefs for yourself tomorrow. You have to start somewhere, but mostly in life we just need to start. It takes time and daily practice that you can do in the morning and the evening. If you do them regularly and with repetition, in time they will become the default setting for you. They will change your life, because what you focus on GROWS. If you focus on the BAD, it will GROW. If you focus on the GOOD it will GROW. If you focus on the DEBT, it will grow. If you focus on your BELLY, it will grow. That which you put your focus on GROWS.

We'll be looking at different practices that I have which are so important to me, and I hope will be important to you too. Remember, what you focus on grows. What you appreciate, APPRECIATES. If you have something in your life that you are feeling really negative about, try to find ways that you can develop an appreciation for that thing, as difficult as that may be. Find ways to do that every day, by writing them down, and you will change your mindset towards them. Change your mindset towards them, you change your energy towards them. You'll find a positive outcome, rather than focusing on the negative energy, for in doing that you'll only find a way for things to end negatively.

The change has to come INSIDE our minds. The change has to come INSIDE our hearts. The change has to come from inside us all. Then, you will change outwardly and so will your circumstances. What happens on the inside will change what happens outside. If you don't change inside of yourself, you'll just be a victim of circumstance, a victim of luck. You can, instead, create the mindset from within that means, whatever happens to you, you will see and create opportunity.

Daily practices are a massive part of the way to be successful in life. They take grit and persistence. Daily practices are the meat and potatoes of fundamental change. Doing things every day in small increments rips up the weeds that were planted by others in your subconscious. New flowers will grow, and from then what you sow you will reap.

Repetition is the key.
Repetition.

Always planting new wonderful belief systems, from this day forward.

What problems do daily practices solve? They tackle your unconscious beliefs that block you from the success that you want to achieve. They slowly but surely change your mindset over time, changing you and creating a new mindset. Whatever you want that mindset to be, daily practices can do that. Daily practices can AND WILL change your self-image. They can change the way you think and respond. They can change the way you react to the world around you, and that causes the world around you to respond differently to you as well. The outcome of this will completely revolutionise the way you think, act and feel in the world.

Accountability

Doing the work every day to change your self-image takes persistence. You must be willing to be very accountable to yourself and take responsibility for your actions. You must be willing to step up and say 'I really WANT this.' It's like going to the gym, you have to do this religiously. You have to do it all the time until it's just like brushing your teeth, it's just automatic.

Now we turn to what I consider one of life's miracles. The miracle of the morning. Getting up in the morning and being able to focus on gratitude, meditation and journaling should become a huge part of your life. I could not now imagine my life without my morning routine; trust me, your whole world can, and will, change. These miracles are the by-product of a new way of living and a new way of life. These routines and practices definitely saved my life, removing a lot of anxiety, and continue to do so daily.

This isn't, however, an overnight, instant miracle. We don't get ourselves into a mess overnight and we don't fix things overnight, either. Rarely in life does success happen without some kind of growth, awareness and self-development. By doing daily practices every day, you are developing as a person. Because you are developing as a person, you will see opportunities and new ways of life that will come up for you. It will just happen. It happened to me; writing a book is not something I never saw coming, but the growth I have gained from it is incredible. Having a huge hairdressing community that counts on me brings me such joy and inner strength. These achievements are really a consequence of living a certain way. They are a consequence of my daily practices. For me, it's centred around the miracle of the morning. All successful people have morning practices, they have disciplines that they follow every day.

When you do these morning practices, over time you will look back and reflect on how much you have changed. It is so important that you follow these morning rituals, these daily practices. They've made me successful and helped me to become the person that I am today; I very much want them to have this transformational impact on your life, whatever it is that YOU want to do and be.

YOU must change YOUR life, one morning at a time. REAL success will come by using self-development to elevate yourself by undertaking daily practices every single day and revolutionising your entire approach to living.

Every morning I like to write out a list of gratitude. Gratitude is very closely linked to miracles. In stating the things that you have already, in the present, just to be thankful for things such as the coffee you are drinking, this is the start of the brain dump of gratitude that you need to write down. Saying it isn't enough, you don't feel it that way. By writing it down you get to feel the emotion. Write down the word 'coffee' and you can imagine yourself with a cup of Starbucks, you can feel it. Feeling is the secret. You must FEEL something first if you want to bring it into your life. This is crucial to understand.

Gratitude is the first daily practice that I do. Writing out the list of things that I am grateful for. They can be the smallest things. You could be grateful for birdsong, grateful for your wife and children, or your husband and children, your wealth, health and happiness, you could be grateful for friends, your salon, your clients or your online community. I'm so used to doing gratitude lists that I can reel them off easily and freely. It is such a beautiful start to my day and it is something I feel every day of my life. I can't describe the magic it creates.

Gratitude won't immediately make your life into a Walt Disney movie, but by practising gratitude every morning you will align your brain to what you HAVE. What you are GRATEFUL for. What you focus on GROWS, as we already know. What you are grateful for expands and you will find that you just have more things to be grateful for. After about six months of doing this, I found myself writing out a full page every day. I had SO much to be grateful for. It changed my life and it changed my health.

Start with what you are grateful for, keep it nice and simple, but do it every day and your brain will get used to it. Think of it as jogging for your mind. This is the first daily practice and nothing attracts magic and miracles into your life more than the feeling and expression of gratitude.

Be grateful, write it down, get it on paper.

Daily practices give you an opportunity to play a part in the success of your future. Every morning there is an opportunity for you to create your new story. To be able to understand that you are worthy of, and able to create, WEALTH, HEALTH, and HAPPINESS.

You MUST start each day becoming the person you want to be that day, not the person you were the day before. Even if yesterday was an amazing day, you must start today as the new person you want to become going forward. It feels really good, it will help you and your life's purpose will come up to the light. Your health will improve and your authentic self will come up. You'll be able to pinpoint belief systems and ways of thinking that have you living in the past, which are blocking you from achieving everything that you want to achieve. You will be able to see the difference between who you are authentically, which is way more than you can imagine, and who you think you are.

There's a huge relationship between early rising and long-term happiness. It's been scientifically proven. Make the changes for yourself inside yourself, don't think life will do it for you. These can be harsh lessons to learn, but they are worth learning. Be the leader in your life! By getting up and doing these exercises, in time, you'll really look forward to getting up in the morning. You'll enjoy every moment as you guide the ship of your life. These practices are the lighthouse of your new day, your new amazing life.

If you want to create success in life, you must meet her halfway. By doing that, success is created through your MINDSET, through your FOCUS, through your FEELINGS. Do this in the first hour of every day and success will chase YOU.

Only five per cent of people in the world will ever do anything like this. The other ninety-five per cent will talk about it and then find a reason to not do it. BE in the five per cent, not the other ninety-five, waiting for life to create something for them. In one to two months of doing this, you can completely change your life. You'll need a telescope to look back at how far you've come.

If you've watched the sun come up, at any time in your life, you can feel that there is a special energy. It holds a unique connection to the universe You have the opportunity to do that every day, the opportunity to develop that feeling inside yourself. That connection. And you can start it today. Start it today and set yourself up for the type of success that you are looking for.

Don't turnover in the bed again once you wake up. If you do that you are turning away from the universe, from the gift of a new day. If you do that you separate yourself from nature and all its wonders, the **VERY** thing that can make **MIRACLES** happen in your life. The very thing that can make connections and change happen in your life. Everything around us is here to help us, but we must connect with it. Connect to the right frequency on the radio station. The number one way to do this is to be up with the sun. Up for that moment of silence, connection and the attitude of gratitude. Every day is an opportunity to connect with the source, connect with everything around you. It may sound simple but it can profoundly change your life, as it has profoundly changed mine.

A Little Warning

You'll come up against objections when you do this type of work. You'll feel the fear and the dread; remember those are the very voices that are keeping you exactly where you are, in your cage. If you fail to make time for your vision and your personal development, you'll have to make time every day for the struggle and the stress that your unchanged life will bring. Unchanged, unlived, unfocused. Days that don't have any dreams or structure in them can turn into un-lived weeks, months, years and lifetimes. This is YOUR life, your chance. Please take it and allow yourself to dream, to create an extraordinary life. Get up out of that bed with a purpose, as you did as a child when you saw the blue sky, it was your birthday and you bounced out singing. We are going to try to create that for you every single day of your life.

Journaling

Journaling HELPS us understand our lives. It creates clarity and space, capturing ideas on paper so that you can see them again. Look back in a year and see your progress. Journaling is like the keyboard to a magic Google, connecting you to the universe early in the morning. It's addictive but in a good way. Commit to it. Get a beautiful journal and use it as part of your morning routine and ritual that will change your life.

Each person is different. For some it's a physical start to the day, for others an intellectual one, for others emotional, others again spiritual.

Life is made up of these four elements, the physical, the intellectual, the emotional and the spiritual. In that first hour of every day, if you can, fill them all up. We've all been programmed with good and bad things in this life, but listen carefully; we don't get what we want, we just get what we believe. So change that belief system inside and build those good habits leading to great living. Each and every day.

Daily Practices

1.   Get Up

Get up, open the curtains and welcome the universe into your life. Have a big stretch or go out into nature for a walk. Feel the breeze on your face. The itch between your toes. You may not have the feet of an athlete, but you may have athlete's foot. Have a large glass of warm water when you get up. Put some lemon in it, if that's your thing; it helps your spleen. No coffee yet, but later is okay.

2.   Gratitude List

Write at least ten things that you are grateful for. Doesn't matter how big or small they are. Could be your brother, bank account or bed.

3. Achievement List

Take an A4 piece of paper and run a line down the middle of it. On one side write the things that you have achieved in your life. On the other side, write down what's going to happen. Here's mine from the morning:

'I am writing this chapter; I am an award-winning and successful salon owner; I am an award-winning and successful colourist; I am a mentor; I am a global ambassador; I am a father; I am a husband; I am a house owner; I am a car owner; I am an entrepreneur; I am a creator; I am the founder of a global hair community online; I am a coach I am a mentor.'

Now, on the other side of the line write down 'What's Going To Happen?' For example:

'I am going to be the author of a published book; I am becoming a REALLY successful coach; A global leader; A multi-multi-millionaire; I am going to help to make a difference; I am going to change the world and make it a better place; I am going to travel the world.'

By putting down what you have achieved, you are reinforcing your self-image of all of the things that you've done already. No matter how big or how small they are, YOU have achieved them. Father, mother, wife, hair stylist, you are already a success. By putting down what is going to happen, you are giving your brain the chance to go and find evidence that they are going to happen. This is magic.

4.   Send Love

Sit, close your eyes and send love to three people. Three people in your life that, for whatever reason, you want to send love to. Write three things about those people that you are sending love to. For example, I could send love to my wife. She is loyal, she is caring and she is such a special person. If I wanted to send some love to my dad, I could think about how he was smart, he was funny and he was charismatic. If I wanted to send love to my eldest brother, Gregory, I would think about how he is a wonderful supporting mentor, he gives intelligent advice and he is a great person.

Give yourself an hour in the morning for these four steps.

Here's one for advanced mornings when you've time and hunger for more. I call this one 'My Perfect Day':

'I've just stepped off my private jet, mobbed by all these amazing people, having flown in from Spain after giving a keynote speech in The Park, Barcelona. One-hundred-thousand people were there to see me and I gave a speech about personal transformation. I changed one-hundred-thousand lives at The Park and then I did a 'Live from Barcelona' live broadcast to thousands more, before changing into my monogrammed cashmere onesie and slipping into the limo that was taking me to my private plane.'

Your perfect day should be way bigger than mine above. Just go wild! Give your brain freedom to dream because it will break free, through our belief systems, and you will be released to go off and make those dreams happen. I'd better start looking for a great pilot for my private jet!

What you have above is a framework that will change your life
beautifully and fairly effortlessly. Do it every morning knowing I am sitting beside you doing mine, and watch your life change so beautifully!

Here's to the future,
Andrew

SECRET 7 - MAGIC AND MIRACLES

This chapter is about all the magic and miracles in life because you can never have enough of them and they are everywhere in this world. Think about the Earth and the fact that it is positioned in the perfect place in proximity to the sun so that it can power us and help everything grow, with a miraculous ozone layer that protects us from outside sources. We have this magical thing called oxygen that we can breathe and renew every day. We have all of these things around us and to just think that they are random is nigh on impossible to imagine. From something chaotic to this elegance? The air that you breathe, the plants that grow, everything here is so finely balanced and beautifully put together. All of it is orchestrated to create LIFE. A life that we get to LIVE.

We get to breathe oxygen, eat the vegetables that we have grown, and walk amongst them if we choose. With that level of understanding and gratitude for your life, it is through the eyes of abundance, it all comes ALIVE. Not just from a material and personal standpoint, but from the bigger picture standpoint. From the glory of a sunset to the ability to be able to move through this life and meet people. You can believe that things are just chaotic and simply take them for granted OR you can look through eyes of true THANKFULNESS and GRATITUDE. That is when the abundance of life will hit you, be bestowed upon you.

It is up to you to create that bulletproof aura around you, your very own ozone layer. That is the miracle of this life you have and the people that are in it. Then, true abundance will be yours. Remember in life we take it for granted and it can be taken from us. See that beautiful sunset, hear your children's laughter, live the most magical present moment and have the most fulfilling life. Whatever happens to you, this level of awareness will reveal to you all the magic around you, bringing you to the understanding of real life and creating wonderful moments for you all along the way.

Is it all blowing in the wind or is there something else, more elegant at play, in the universe? I believe that there is. Every day I see magic and miracles. You must find that truth for yourself through the power of the universe, your children, yourself as a person. Find that clarity in your life. When you find it, I guarantee you that the abundance you are looking for will be yours. You will find it inside yourself. Put your hand over your heart, do it now, and feel the magic of being alive TODAY. Treasure being able to do the things that you want to do moving forwards. Value the ability to see a sunrise, see a sunset; they are there every day for us. If they were the last two sights we would get to see on the planet today, you'd remember every single second of them. We take them for granted because we think it isn't our last day on the planet. Enjoy them, take in the moment, get up early to see the morning miracle which happens every single day.

Make LIVING the central point of your life. Make gratitude your default setting and you WILL find the happiness you seek. You will, because it already resides inside of you.

There are difficult things and experiences we have all lived through which have left their marks on us but the question is, who is left to drink the poison of all this trauma? Many of us have been through awful abuse, sometimes at the hands of our parents, teachers, loved ones or partners. We hold these memories and scars deep in our hearts, bodies and minds. Yet they only poison US. They do not poison the perpetrator. They have often suffered their own abuse and have just used you as a mirror for their own insecurities, or as part of their own movies of their lives that they are making in their heads. You are often a bit-part player in these movies and it's not until your later years that you realise holding onto these things poisons you each and every day. That's a hard thing to accept as we were just victims or just made bad decisions, but it's a complete truth. Test it for yourself. It's a difficult subject I know, it blocked me for so long, but it is one that we all need to overcome if we want to live the life that we want to live. You'll need to learn to find lessons and thankfulness for the WORST circumstances of your life. I know what I'm inviting you to do is so hard; trust me, I had to do it myself. Find the lesson for you, find something to be thankful for, and you will find the way to remove poison from your life. You must heal it to live freely and be in the present, you must.

You CANNOT move forward and see the miracles and magic in this life if you do not heal from your past. If, at the core of your being, there is huge resentment and huge anger, that will just expand and emanate across all areas of your life. It will stop you from being able to be intimate with your partners and stop you from being able to give love to your children. It will stop you from being present, from seeing the sunrise and the sunset, from fully being and living in this world.

Be on the journey that you are absolutely and authentically meant to be on. If you don't do this, you'll just be a passenger in the journey of your life, rather than being the driver of it. You'll be a victim of fate, based on past resentments, rather than being in charge of your own journey.

I invite you, as difficult as this may be, to write down the names of people that maybe you feel have done you wrong, who treated you badly. Those that have caused you serious pain in your life. Think about things that those people have about them that make them worthy. I'll start you off:

I had a difficult maths teacher who I'm going to call Mr L, a very difficult man. Without delving too deeply into the past, I went to a Christian Brothers school. I'll let you imagine the worst of it; it was hell on Earth and I felt completely worthless as a person there. A nothing, less than human. But now, in my life, I've learnt to have gratitude for those days.

So, Mr L, what to say? He taught me maths, and I'm brilliant at maths because of him. He was a man who tried his best. He was definitely somebody who wanted, at the bottom of it all, to make kids the best they could possibly be. He taught me the lesson of living with anxiety and panic attacks, and how to control and overcome them. I was never comfortable in situations and he taught me how to be comfortable with the uncomfortable, how to deal with difficult people in difficult situations, and how to overcome them and make things work in my favour.

I learnt an awful lot from Mr L and I'm grateful for having him in my life, as difficult as it was — and still is, I have to find the lesson in it, I know I have to find the lesson in it. Otherwise, the story stays in my life forever and ever and I would always be the victim That will block ME from living my life, not him.

That kind of thing will block you, too. How much it blocks you, your heart and your soul, is up to you. Remember, you drink the poison. YOU drink the poison and THEY don't even know. As difficult as this may be, you will sit down with certain names and you will not be able to find one single redeeming feature at the start. In time, you will find that, maybe, they were loyal or human. You will find ways. Every time you find something, a little part of you comes back to life. A little part of who you originally were. A little more of your superpower, your presence, your charisma. A little bit more of you comes alive for the people around you. For the people around you and for YOU. For your life, for your friendships, for your loved ones, for your kids, for your partner. A little bit more of you will become available. That will bring so much JOY and so much presence into this world because you will become the person that you were originally born to be.

All of these things happened to us all. So, I invite you to sit down and start to FORGIVE. Not for them, but for you. Not just for you, but for everybody in your life. I know this is a difficult thing I am asking, I'm holding your hand and with all the love in the world, I say this. It is not how we felt in those horrible moments that determine our lives, it is how we deal with them NOW. That is all that matters. Make it right in your mind and your heart today, and remember, life supports you and your belief system whether it is good or bad for you.

Think of it as the yin and yang of life, such that there is night and day in every life. The tide comes in and it goes out again. Life is not all one tone. It has contrast, light and shade. Duality. Tears and joy. When you feel these difficult feelings, it usually means that the other end of the spectrum is coming. If we are going through difficult times, know that the opposite duality has to happen. What goes up, must come down. What goes down must come back up. When you are down you are going to go back up. That is one hundred percent guaranteed. You see this with the vibrations of music, with the tides, in and out. The laws of nature. Its the miracle of life

Be confident that when you are experiencing a downtime, the UP times are coming. Be ready for big breakthroughs. I know it is so difficult to wait for them, I know it's hard. I know that your own brain is telling you that this has been a core of who you are. This is my STORY, it is the reason why I am allowed to fail. It is the reason that I'm allowed to stay in bed late. It is the reason that I drink more than I should drink or eat more than I should eat, because of the victimhood I've gone through in my life.

It's when you think you can't do things in life, that's when you absolutely MUST. push forward and do them. You MUST take action and the changes you yearn for will come in your life. I promise you. They will come, sometimes quickly, sometimes slowly, but you will look back and see how different things were before. In a good way.

Always keep this book beside your bed. Keep it close and trust me, you will look back in a year's time and the past traumas will have melted from your life. They will just be a picture that comes up in your unconscious, an abuser or whomever, and there will be no emotional resonance attached to that picture. It will just be like a cloud that goes by in your life. You've found the secret sauce, you've found the superpower, the miracles and magic that are everywhere in your life. Even the ones you don't totally understand at first will come to you in time.

You are supported, you are loved,
Andrew

SECRET 8 - GRATITUDE

We are all addicted to the old self, the old habits, the stuff that has got us into this mess. To start with, this journey is like a honeymoon with our road set out before us. But as we make some progress and start to change, we will meet resistance. Nothing in this world wants to die and that includes your old self. This can feel quite unbearable at times but it is to be expected and prepared for, something that you have to walk through because change is a requirement and change is TOUGH.

So after the honeymoon period, you may feel:

Stage 1: strong resistance and a little unbearable

Stage 2: UNCOMFORTABLE

Yes, it's uncomfortable and it stays so, but you get comfortable with the uncomfortable. Then, LITTLE BY LITTLE, YOU START WINNING THE BATTLE. You must keep going. Because...

Stage 3: YOU WILL START TO FEEL UNBEATABLE. !!!!

When you start to feel unbeatable, you'll look back and say, 'Oh my God, I have an absolutely new life!' All of this can be done in thirty to sixty days. The rewards are waiting for you on the other side. Expect it to be unbearable, know it is going to be uncomfortable, but know that you are going to become unbeatable.

Let today be the day that you walk away from all that you have BEEN all these years and towards who you are about to BECOME, the you that you are meant to be. Remember, things don't change in life until WE change. When we take action our life changes immediately around us. this is a scientific fact. So, waiting for life to change around you so that you can have everything you want will just not happen. It WILL NOT happen. You BE the change today and create the opportunities, courage and awareness that will create the attitude …

The ATTITUDE of GRATITUDE.

Life will change automatically for you. Remember to be grateful for what you have today, accept what you don't have and then create what you want from there. You can do this from TODAY. Understand that being unsatisfied and unhappy are two different things. I, for example, am unhappy with my weight, I have a big belly that I need to lose, but I am still happy with myself. I'm happy that I'm on the journey towards what I need. Maybe I need to put weight loss at the top of my list of the things that I drive forward, but that's deep inside myself.

You can be deeply happy AND yet still deeply unsatisfied. It is quite alright, life is full of duality. You can be very happy with what you have and also know that what you want to create is coming towards you at the right time and place. You are now the creator in your life, on your journey of creation. That's the default setting you want. People have a habit because they are unhappy with their results today, they link that to their long-term goals and happiness and it blocks them; you must separate the two.

You can be extremely happy with what you have and yet still want more. There's nothing wrong with that, it's quite normal. Do NOT get the two mixed up in your life. Happiness and satisfaction are two completely different things. Be happy today to create the satisfaction that is coming towards you tomorrow. This is the understanding needed for your creation of success.

Morning Rituals - The Core

The aptly named 'first thing' you need to be able to do is to get up early. First thing, in fact. There are many rituals that we will go through, but the first one is written strategies. They work automatically. It's very good to have a journal and pen, or a phone that you are happy with. These are the things that you can use to train your mind and find the positive in life, every day.

To a certain extent, the brain is always set on the perceived threat and negative focus, only because it is always afraid of you failing or hurting yourself by getting rejected. The brain has a very old part that is triggered by any threat and tries to protect you. It doesn't care about your success, happiness or achievements, it just cares about protecting you. You need to love that part of the brain, the old part that's protecting you from the sabre-toothed tiger, and understand that it isn't out to get you, it doesn't hate you, it just wants to keep you alive. If it could keep you in a room, doors locked, your jailer bringing your food, it would be delighted. But you wouldn't have much of a life, would you?

You need to retrain your brain and open different pathways up so that you can recreate the future that you are looking for and let go of the past. Let the brain get into sleepy mode and overcome it. The number one thing for this is a moment's silence first thing in the morning. Open the curtains, take a breath, get a glass of water and get onto the number one thing for you … a gratitude list.

Gratitude expands your life, opens you up to miracles and allows you to feel blessed for all that you already have in your life. It is the special sauce of life. Practising gratitude helps you to focus on the positive things already in your life, leaving you open and ready to welcome more of the good things as they come your way.

Write down ten to fifteen things that you are grateful for. Right now I am very grateful for my wife, my family, my health, my savings, my house, my car, my morning coffee, my mentors, my coaches, my salon, my salon team, my house, my car and my clothes I'm wearing. The items on your list can be as big or small as you want them to be. It's not the size you're looking for, it's the feeling behind it. It's about the expression and expansion of our gratitude.

Even if you just did this every day as your only practice, it would build up a level of gratitude that would lead on to greater things. This book tells us that what we focus on grows and what we appreciate, appreciates. Gratitude is at the centre of everything in life. It opens the doors to the kingdom of wealth and happiness.

So, the gratitude list is the first of the morning rituals. It's at the centre of this book and is a simple way that you can create positivity and pass it on. You can pass it on to your children, with a phrase such as 'Tell me what you are grateful for today.' Kids give you things like Mum and Dad, Teacher, Nando's … it teaches them a level of gratitude that THEY can pass on, a way of life.

It's like prayer and a signal to the universe, being so grateful for what you have. It creates more of what you want. There's nothing like the feeling of being thankful, nothing. It heals so much and so quickly, but it must be practised every day.

Gratitude, far from being airy-fairy, as some would have it, is one of the most important things that you can do. Defaulting the brain towards finding your blessings. That's just so powerful. Think about it; pretty much anybody who is reading this book is living in the top ten per cent. Look back at the other ninety per cent, so many of whom are very poor and very sadly less well off. The opportunities for them to invest in themselves and better themselves are very scarce. Just taking it at that level means that, as readers of this book, who can read, with a light on, heating ourselves, we need to count our blessings and count them daily.

9 SECRETS TO A MEANINGFUL LIFE

When judging yourself, always look back and see how far you've come. Have gratitude just for that. If you are reading this book, you are blessed. You have time on your hands to be able to invest in the most important thing in your life. YOU. Your happiness and your confidence.

Put the book down now for a moment, and see how blessed and lucky you are. You are already in the top ten per cent of this world and you are INVESTING in yourself. You are awesome!

I'm dyslexic, so the word gratitude is very vowel-y and sometimes doesn't feel right so I often use the word THANKS instead. Just giving thanks and giving praise is all that is needed. The thing to remember is that it isn't the word you use that matters, it's how it makes you FEEL which is the key to discovering happiness. That is what you need for a deeply meaningful life.

Feeling is the key to everything. Gratitude makes you feel a connection with the world. Remember how you felt as a kid? On Christmas Eve, looking at the baubles and the flashing fairy lights, getting ready for Santa to come. That feeling that you had inside on your birthday, or going away on holiday with your family. That energy you felt inside, that feeling: that's GRATITUDE.

NOW is the time. Try to find that feeling inside yourself right now. Remember what you were like as a kid; playing, climbing, talking to your pets, cuddling your teddies, how you felt then is the essence of gratitude. That's what will help you find gratitude in yourself. Once you've found that, you need to give some level of gratitude for where you have been in the past compared to where you are today. You need to be able to make amends with the past and the present, and be comfortable with that. What's forgotten about in life is that what we take for granted, will be taken from us. What we take for granted decreases, ever so slowly, until we don't notice at all that it's gone.

When you have that feeling of the six-year-old you and the gratitude you felt back then, you need to sit down and make out a list. A list of the areas in which your gratitude is growing and the areas in which your gratitude is shrinking. For example, let's look at MONEY. Look at the results in your life around money, but not in a feeling kind of way — we'll get to that later. Is your money increasing, or is it decreasing? Your gratitude towards money perhaps needs to change.

How is your HEALTH? Your diet, your exercise routine. Is your internal gratitude working for your health?

How are your RELATIONSHIPS? With your partner, with your workmates. How is your gratitude in those areas of your life?

How is HOME? How is the energy in your home, how's the VIBE? How much do you love where you live? What things are going on there?

How about where you WORK? Is there a sense of gratitude from you towards your workplace, a sense of happiness about it?

How about your STUDIES? I'm well known for putting great emphasis on study. It's very important to me. How are your studies going?

Thinking about all of the above and more, which areas are blooming and which are shrinking? You'll be able to spot quite quickly which areas you need to work on. This list is SO important and it needs to be adjusted all of the time. It's about spinning plates. While writing this book, I have perhaps taken my family and the salon for granted. Gratitude has decreased in both areas and by making my list, I can see that I need to increase my gratitude towards them both. I need to sit down and work out why I LOVE the salon, love the team, what each person brings to the table and how lucky I am to be able to give service to people. By looking at it and talking about it, that's how gratitude grows. It's the same with my family, my wife and children. It's SO important to be able to work these lists, to understand if gratitude is shrinking it's nobody's fault but your own and always remember what we take for granted will be taken from us. If you want to receive, you must give. Giving starts with gratitude and you must give with thanks.

The more you do this, the more you will feel gratitude grow. Practice giving thanks and the more you do it, the more it will grow. Gratitude will grow and your life will CHANGE. Remember, the key here is not the words themselves, it's about feeling. Feel the thanks, taste it, hold it, and live by it.

The more you do it, the easier it will get and the more you will feel.

Once you've done this, you can be really clear about what you want in life. You can sit down and make a list of what you REALLY want out of life. Focus on what you really want, who you want to be, what you want to do and what you want to have. What do you want from YOUR life? Do you want to be a millionaire, win awards, and have a great title? What do you want to be? A great father, a professional sportsperson? What do you want to stand for? What is your LEGACY going to be? Look at these things, make a list: health, relationships, money, work, career, education, study, travel, cars, awards, and achievements. What do you wanna be, do, or have? It's your life. How do you feel? How much do you want to earn? This list will change over time.

To give you a bit of an idea, let's look at our health and ways of bringing gratitude into that aspect of your life. It's hard to understand gratitude without actually seeing it. So let me consider my arms and hands. They have enabled me to create a career for myself. I've been able to do beautiful colour with them. They enable me to hold the hands of my children, touch somebody's face and tell them I love them. I'm able to write this. I'm able to draw. I'm able to throw shapes when I dance. Do you see how much gratitude I must have for my arms and hands?

My legs have been with me from the get-go and they enable me to run, dance and move. I can go downstairs right now and make a cuppa. I can step out after that cuppa and take a walk, feel the air on my face … THIS is what it means to have gratitude. It's a feeling, and one of the most important feelings in the world.

My eyes, while I'm out on that walk, enable me to see this wonderful world. See that sunrise, really look at it. To see that rising sun is such a blessing. If it was your last sunrise you would drink it right in, so live it like it is! With my eyes, I am able to see the beautiful faces of my children. I'm able to see the wonderful hair colours that I do. It is all around me. It is all around you. Gratitude for the things we take for granted, such as our eyes, legs, arms, hands... our ears... just this weekend I was listening to some amazing music. To be able to LISTEN to that music with my ears, to be able to communicate, to listen to the wind and the birds in the morning. I am just SO blessed. So grateful to have these things in my life. See how quickly this grows inside you.

I am so grateful to have a voice that I can use to talk with and to sing with, a mouth that I can smile with and can taste with. I have so much to be grateful for. So much that I am in danger of taking it for granted, as we all are.

Let us all think about our HEARTS that pump blood around our bodies. They keep us alive twenty-four hours a day. They never stop working for us. Our hearts are just the most incredible machines. I'm so grateful for my heart and can feel the gratitude rising and rising in me. This is the key.

Consider our MINDS. They are central to how we can grow, how we can change, how we can create, how we can dream, and how we can make a picture. Everything we can see in our minds and feel in our hearts. We can have it in our hands and I know that you can too.

How about the IMAGINATION? Somebody dreamt about being able to fly a plane, going to the moon and creating electricity; they went on and DID it. That's the wonderful thing about being human. We tend to leave our magic and mystery of the imagination behind us at a certain age, not do anything with it and then think our minds work against us when actually it can work for us and create everything we could ever want.

Think about your organs, your skin, your immune system. Think about how much of your health you take for granted. It's scary! You can do this, do gratitude, with each of the things listed above, and watch how what we appreciate just appreciates. Everything from the streets being cleaned in the morning to eating an apple that has flown halfway around the world just for you. Be grateful.

Blessed and grateful are we, to live in this incredible world of abundance. We take it for granted and look for what we don't have. You can never have what you don't have and want until you truly love who you are and what you've already achieved. This is the core of the magic of gratitude. Live it every day and watch your life expand so beautifully.

With thanks to you, dear reader,
Andrew

SECRET 9 - DECISION-MAKING

For most of our lives, we were never really taught how to make decisions. Governments shield us all along the way and our mothers and fathers, out of love, try to protect us and make as many decisions as they possibly can for us. So we grow up with very little understanding of how to make decisions. I know that I did. Therefore, as an adult, I've been able to understand why we often make 'weak' or 'soft' decisions.

'What is one of those?' I hear you ask. It's a decision that isn't going to change your life or change your day. Will I have a Coke, or will I have a Pepsi? Large or small fries? Ice cream or something healthy? Netflix or Amazon Prime? All weak decisions and the big problem is we aren't even very good at making them. Indeed, we often make them totally unconsciously.

Let's look at a weak decision regarding our fitness, for example. You might join the cheapest gym you can find. A twenty euro a week gym that's open 24/7. That's a weak decision. Your investment in yourself is so small that you'll see very minimal benefits from it. A strong decision can affect your life and yourself emotionally. Take the gym; what if you took your fitness seriously and hired the best personal trainer. That PT might cost hundreds of euros, so this kind of strong decision-making will perhaps make you anxious at the start.

But by making a strong decision, committing to invest in the PT and going for it, you are betting on yourself, investing in yourself and dedicating yourself to getting results. This way, you're going to get them.

By making a strong decision and taking decisive action, you'll be emotionally committed, you'll be mentally committed AND you'll be financially committed. This means you'll be on the hook in every way possible. You'll want to see that money return in lost weight, gained fitness and improved health. You'll be up early and running with your PT, and you'll be doing similar exercises to the ones you'd have been doing in the twenty-euro-a-month gym. The difference is the strong decision that you have made and the commitment that you have made to yourself. This kind of decision-making will change your life and revolutionise everything for you.

Strong decisions will feel uncomfortable at first. Making a strong decision to invest in your health, education, personal transformation and development include things such as buying a new house, or investing in a new car; these are all strong decisions. You'll have to invest in strong decisions and accept they will make you uncomfortable, but understand that the difference is in YOU MAKING them. By you making them, you will have committed. That's where the MAGIC lies.

It's not the personal trainer that changed your life in our fitness example, not at all, it's your decision to hire her. Your commitment to getting a result was the thing that made the difference. So, by investing in yourself, putting yourself on the hook, even if it doesn't go your way, you'll learn from it and it will toughen you up.

There's no such thing as a bad decision. There's only NO decision. No decision is a state of paralysis, and this is the place that most people live in. NOTHING gets done. Just decide to get good at making decisions and the resources and people that you need will always turn up. Decision-makers bet on themselves and see success at every turn.

Remember, most of us are completely untrained in this way of making decisions. I only learned to make decisions about what to do in my life in my forties, by going into my own business and putting myself on the hook. Making a commitment to making the salon work. My salon went on to win 'Best Salon of the Year' and so many other awards. Was I nervous? Was I afraid? Absolutely I was. Until I won 'Irish Times Best Retail Award' in 2016. That's when I felt that I had completed that particular journey and reached a milestone, and then I was looking for new goals and taking the decisions, betting on myself, doing the work and making great decisions can be expensive times. Good people don't work for free!

The dream house isn't going to be cheaper than the one you are in. The dream car and holidays come at a price, but all of these things are so well worth it. They are a reflection of how we see ourselves and our self-image. You will feel uncomfortable around strong decision-making, but you MUST get good at it. Bet on yourself, invest in yourself. This year I've been betting on myself with multiple coaches and I barely gave it a thought. I just did it.

I rarely worry about where the money was going to come from during my life, once the decision is made, it just arrives.

It always arrives after you've made the decision. It never arrives before you've made the decision; it's called having faith and belief in yourself. Everything you are looking for is on the other side of the decision. Once you have completely let go and committed, invested and made yourself accountable, put yourself on the hook, it will all happen for you. Until you do that, the outcome will be down to luck or outside circumstances. We can then blame anything else when things don't go our way, instead of ourselves.

Get comfortable with the discomfort of making strong decisions. Know the difference between a weak decision, such as the type of coffee you will have today, and a strong decision, such as knowing where you are going to be in a year from now.

Decision-making is the key.

Stop focusing on things that don't create great results in your life. Living through different fictional and documentary characters does nothing for our lives. The daily news is there to scare you and keep you on your couch. Trust me, take a pass, and forget about it. Think about things you can do that make you feel good. Focus on the things that you want to achieve, that light up your heart.

If you knew you couldn't fail,
well what would you do?
what would you really do with this amazing life?

Focus on your purpose,
Focus on your mission,
Focus on your family,
Focus on giving.
Focus on things that you want to achieve and things you love.
STOP focusing on things that do nothing.
Focus on the results in your life

Feeling Pain is Normal.
Suffering is Not.

Pain is something that comes with the experience of all the things that we go through in life I'm afraid, but suffering is something different, something that we tend to bring upon ourselves by replaying these experiences over and over again. In doing so we create a much bigger story around them. We can create suffering that lasts a whole lifetime. Our whole lives can become determined by that story, sadly. The answer lies in us learning from the experience, taking away the lessons for growth and using that pain to uplift and serve other people. Not doing so will affect our self-image and our opportunity to be happy and successful.

Painful experiences are normal, but most suffering, I'm afraid, is self-inflicted. At some stage, we have to take responsibility for that, remove the suffering, remove the story, and remember the experience but remove the pain. Use the lesson to serve and help other people. This is what I have done in my life and it's a powerful secret.

I CAN

Our mindset of 'I CAN' is way more important than your IQ ever will be. To be an effective leader you must be able to go first, be able to make decisions quickly and cover the ground fast and swiftly. Remember, there's no such thing as a bad decision. The only bad decision you'll make is the one you don't make. You'll learn from it, course correct and get back to your goal. For people to be led by you, follow you, how you feel and what you create must come from YOU. It's only your vision that will light up other people.

We all can replay stories of trauma and all that it does is recharge the trauma again, stronger every time. Doing this, living in the story, makes it very difficult to be happy or successful in our lives. In this way, we can never get away from our stories. Each experience is only really a lesson that we can go through and we must learn the lesson each time. The lessons are usually small ones. Somebody who didn't love us. Somebody casting judgement on us, who was most likely more damaged than we ever were. There are usually straightforward lessons to be learned, but when we relive these stories we recharge them again and again over the years. They become the most horribly pent-up emotions. I know this from experience. Sometimes these emotions can knock you on your back! It's hard, I know, but we must stand still and let them hit us.

Allowing ourselves to experience our stories can be rough at times, throwing up pent-up, repressed emotions, but remember they won't kill us. If we can do this, it will be the last time we have to do it. Then we can learn the lesson and we can let the pain go.

Here's the thing ...
you are NOT the story,
and you never were xx

Experience it, feel it, learn the lesson,
and let it go forever.

Create your tomorrow today,
instead of blaming yesterday for today.

Time to take chances, create big goals, and live the life of the person you were always supposed to be. There's an incredible person inside you trying to get out. That person is the real you. Stand still, let it hit you. It won't be easy, but once you've done it and you're out the other side, you'll have learned the lesson and you'll never have to go through it again. That pain will no longer be your story and another part of you will come back to life. In no time it will be just you living in your present and no longer your story, creating amazing experiences for yourself.

AND FINALLY ...
IF YOU ARE LIVING THEN YOU NEED TO BE
LEARNING
IN LIFE.
IF YOU WANT TO BE EARNING, YOU MUST BE
LEARNING !!
We are either growing
or sadly fading in our lives.
We must continue to move towards being the best we can be
in this wonderful gift of life
Right up until the minute your time comes to leave it,
but there is no standing still,
so don't waste a second of it,
you can make the choice today

Remember you are way more
in every way than you know,
so live it with all your heart.

    All my love always,
    Andrew

EPILOGUE

Thank you so much for taking the time to read my book. A lot of the concepts here take a little time to grasp and become a way of life, so my advice would be to pick a chapter to read and work on every day for a month, then pick another, and so on. Just go with what is relevant to you at the time.

Life is for living! We are either fading or growing in this beautiful world we are blessed to get to be a part of, and if we choose to continue to grow, life will reward us with so many blessings. So don't waste a second of it. Live and give with all your heart, and know that you are valued way more than you will ever know.

Love,
Andrew

Cover photo by Nadine Reid

Story Terrace

Printed in Poland
by Amazon Fulfillment
Poland Sp. z o.o., Wrocław
26 July 2023